STRENGTH BEAUTY SPIRIT

Images of the Mohonk Preserve and Shawangunk Ridge

1. Late Autumn Afternoon, Lake Awosting

STRENGTH BEAUTY SPIRIT

Images of the Mohonk Preserve and Shawangunk Ridge

G. Steve Jordan

CE

CLOVE EDITIONS

Stone Ridge, New York

To Joanne & Bill —

G. Steve Jordan

Oct 22 2003

To my parents and for Ann

STRENGTH BEAUTY SPIRIT
*Images of the Mohonk Preserve
and Shawangunk Ridge*

First Edition.
Photographs and text © G. Steve Jordan 2003

Book Design: Amy Hecht

Fine art prints of images in this book are available.

Please refer to the book index for the image number

or visit www.mohonkimages.com.

Paragraph 1 on page 13 from HOLY THE FIRM

by Annie Dillard. Copyright © Annie Dillard

Reprinted by permission of HarperCollins

Publishers, Inc.

Library of Congress Catalog Card Number:
2003093336

ISBN: 0-9720366-0-1

Published by
Clove Editions, P.O. Box 840, Stone Ridge, NY 12484

2. Late Autumn Along the Peterskill OPPOSITE

3. Sunrise, Awosting Falls

4. Sky Top and Thistle, Butterville Road FOLLOWING, PAGES 8 AND 9

G. Steve Jordan's images invite us not only to view the world, but to marvel at its moments of grace. His photographs combine a joyful serendipity with an artist's passion for placement, form and color. Steve's deep appreciation of the remarkable Shawangunk Ridge is communicated throughout these pages. In each image, the photographer's profound respect for, and celebration of, his surroundings is evident.

Thank you, Steve, for sharing with us these "found moments." Each one tells a tale of its own and invites viewers to experience the setting in a visceral way. Those who know and love the Shawangunk Ridge as one of the "last great places" in the world will have a sense of coming home as they peruse these pages. Those who are discovering the area for the first time will delight in its timeless grace...a touchstone in a world where such healing is needed now more than ever.

Nina Smiley, Mohonk Mountain House

Located less than a hundred miles from the concrete canyons of New York City and within a half-day's drive of over 20 million people, the Shawangunk Mountains have been designated by the Nature Conservancy as "One of the Last Great Places on Earth." Encompassing a particularly beautiful section of the Shawangunk Ridge, the 6,400-acre Mohonk Preserve is an exhilarating expanse of varied landscapes. Crevices more than a hundred feet deep slice through solid rock, in places creating a labyrinth of tunnels and narrow passageways. Bare rock plateaus, crystal clear glacially-formed lakes, and pristine streams, cascades and waterfalls are among the cherished features of this area. Alongside these natural resources are lush wooded slopes, open fields, and rich wetlands. Rare species of plants and animals call this region home — a recent study found 36 distinct natural plant communities in the northern Shawangunks alone. Geologic and climatic factors combine to make the Ridge a meeting place where both northern and southern ranging species can be found. Migrating hawks, vultures, and eagles make use of uplifting warm air thermals rising from this rugged topography to aid their flight. As a result, it is a key migration route.

GEOLOGY

The rocks that form the Shawangunks were created over 420 million years ago. Sediments were deposited in shallow braided streams where heat and pressure later compressed this quartz-rich silt into tremendously hard and durable rocks. The resulting Shawangunk Conglomerate erodes very slowly, is quite brittle, and tends to crack and break away in large sections, forming crevices, ice caves, and the brilliant white cliffs we admire today. During the last Ice Age, vast glaciers thousands of feet thick covered the area. These glaciers scraped soil and rock from the ridgetop, smoothed and polished exposed rock surfaces, and gouged out huge basins that later filled with melted ice, forming stunningly clear sky lakes.

THE HUMAN INFLUENCE

Prehistoric humans first arrived in the area almost 11,000 years ago as the glaciers were retreating. One of the first places in the region to be free of ice, the Shawangunks attracted small bands of wandering Native American hunting parties who came to hunt, trap, and gather berries and nuts, often following the ridgetop as a route of migration and trade.

The earliest European settlers arrived over 350 years ago and spread throughout the area, clearing the forests as they went. These early residents held utilitarian view that the land existed strictly as a resource to meet their needs for food, clothing and trade goods. Many believed they had a "noble mission" — that untamed wilderness was chaotic and profane and that by clearing and farming the land they were civilizing it.

Construction of the Delaware & Hudson Canal in 1828 transformed the region from a rural backwater, introducing industrial development, commercialization, and population growth. After harvesting the Ridge for timber, the canal provided the settlers

5. Winter Reflections, Wallkill River

a means for transporting this valuable commodity to urban markets. Eventually, small numbers of settlers moved onto land that had been cleared, establishing mountain communities that revolved around farming and grazing, timber and charcoal production, the manufacture of barrel hoops and millstones and other cottage industries.

LAND AS INSPIRATION

By the 19th century, humans' relationship to nature began to undergo an important change. Many came to idealize wilderness, believing that experiencing the natural environment firsthand might help relieve the physical and mental distress that was a byproduct of a modern urban lifestyle. At about this time, the Romantic Movement spread to America's shores from Europe. Romantics equated nature with spirituality. The 19th century's urban elite flocked to resorts high in the mountains, like Mohonk Mountain House and the hotels at Minnewaska Lake, where the scenery was beautiful, the air fresh, the environment pristine, and the stresses fewer.

ACCESS AND PRESERVATION

Resort development would not have occurred so dramatically had it not been for the development of the rail system in the 1870's. Proximity to rail lines meant that the Shawangunks, and Mohonk in particular, were within a day's journey from New York City for the first time. Today, thousands visit the "Gunks" each year, making this the most popular climbing destination east of the Mississippi. Wonderful scenery, easy access, an infrastructure of roads and parking areas, and a superb network of trails, plus maps, guides, and other published literature, all help account for its growing popularity with hikers, mountain bikers and urban residents seeking the same tranquility and beauty enjoyed by their 19th century predecessors.

Paralleling these newfound and growing strains on the land, efforts to preserve the Shawangunks and protect the Ridge from development and abuse have grown as well. In 1963, the Mohonk Trust, later renamed the Mohonk Preserve, was created to manage and protect land formerly owned by Mohonk Mountain House. The Mohonk Preserve has since been active in acquiring adjacent properties to enhance the integrity of the Ridge. In addition to the Mohonk Preserve, groups like The Nature Conservancy, Open Space Institute, Friends of the Shawangunks, and Palisades Interstate Park Commission are involved in local land preservation.

As a unique, universal place, the Shawangunks merit our enjoyment and protection.

Jeffrey Perls is the author of "The Shawangunks Trail Companion."

6. Wild Azalea, Awosting Falls

7. Evening Catskill Profile, from North Lookout Carriageway FOLLOWING PAGE

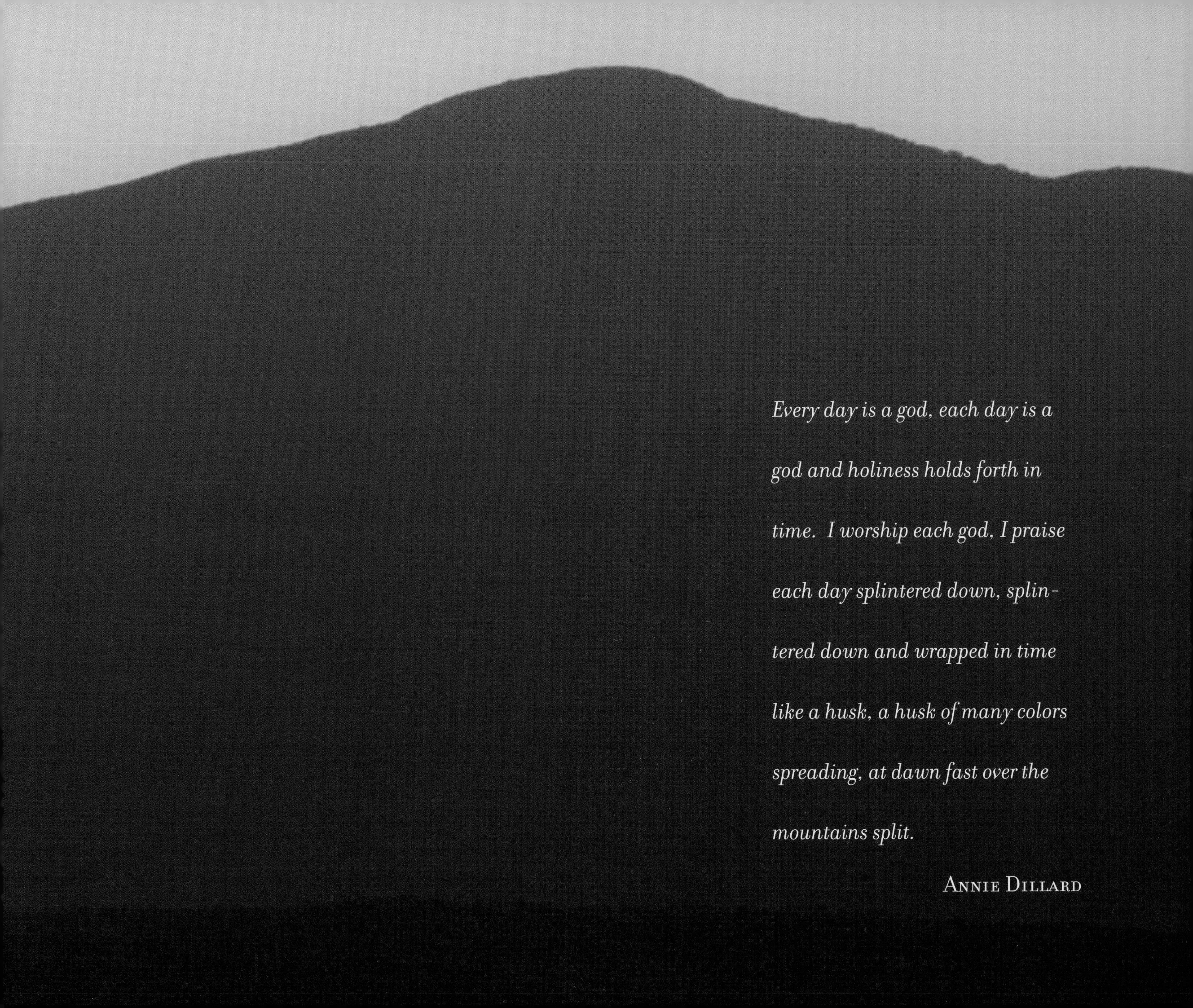

Every day is a god, each day is a

god and holiness holds forth in

time. I worship each god, I praise

each day splintered down, splin-

tered down and wrapped in time

like a husk, a husk of many colors

spreading, at dawn fast over the

mountains split.

ANNIE DILLARD

STRENGTH

8. Autumn Copes View PRECEDING PAGE, LEFT

9. After The Storm, Orchard Pond

If you do not expect it, you will not find

the unexpected, for it is hard to find and

difficult.

HERACLITUS

10. Autumn, Chapel Farm

11. Autumn, Split Rock OPPOSITE

One of photography's unique strengths, compared to other artistic media, is its ability to isolate and record a precise instant in time. We may think we've seen or experienced a particular feature of a landscape — a field or forest — forgetting that a landscape exists not only as a geographic location, but also as a discrete moment in the flow of eternity. The two images here, taken from the same location, reflect how utterly different a scene may appear when captured at separate moments.

12. Summer, Coxing Kill

13. Winter, Coxing Kill OPPOSITE

14. Sunrise and Daisy Along Butterville Road

The air, as soon as it is light, is filled with innumerable images

to which the eye serves as a magnet.

LEONARDO DA VINCI

15. Wallkill View Barn

16. Above Awosting Falls

17. Autumn Sunset Above the Clove

18. Morning Fog FOLLOWING PAGE LEFT

19. Summer Morning, Humpo Marsh FOLLOWING PAGE, RIGHT

20. Queen Anne's Lace, Sky Top

21. Jumbled Boulders, Eagle Cliff

22. Dusk, Along Gatehouse Road

23. Winter Sunset, Below Split Rock

24. Winter Detail, Below Eagle Cliff

Everybody needs beauty as well as bread, places to play in and pray in, where Nature may heal and cheer and give strength to body and soul alike.

JOHN MUIR

25. Fiddleheads

26. Ledge Detail, Rock Rift

27. Woodland, Near Duck Pond OPPOSITE

28. Autumn Sun Through Maples

In seeking to interpret the landscape, the artist encounters a dichotomy between exploration and realization. A certain measure of discipline must be exercised in pursuit of an often ambiguous objective. Yet that same discipline must be abandoned to allow impressions of each landscape to percolate into one's consciousness in a manner consistent with the land-scape itself, rather than a preconceived idea of what the landscape is or should be.

The images on this page were realized only after I had given up trying to capture the autumn colors as I expected to find them. Only then, it seemed, did I release my notions of autumn and become receptive to the scenes that were before me all the time.

29. Autumn Reflections OPPOSITE

30. Autumn Saplings, Boulder

31. Talus Slope, Below Sky Top

32. Along Jenny Lane Trail

33. Summer Sunrise

34. Autumn, Lower Coxing Kill

35. Awosting Falls, Ferns

36. Stony Kill Falls

37. Spring Reflections FOLLOWING PAGE, LEFT

38. Winter Afternoon, Near Split Rock FOLLOWING PAGE, RIGHT

39. Rock Rift

40. Mountain Laurel Blooms, Birches

41. Sky Top Spring, #2 FOLLOWING PAGE

Objects are concealed from our view, not
so much because they are out of the
course of our visual ray as because we do
not bring our minds and eyes to bear on
them. The greater part of the phenomena
of Nature are for this reason concealed
from us all our lives.

HENRY DAVID THOREAU

42. Autumn Leaf Detail

43. Autumn Blueberry Bushes

44. Summer Stream Detail, Lower Coxing Kill FOLLOWING PAGE, LEFT

45. Coxing West Spring FOLLOWING PAGE, RIGHT

I am following Nature without being able to

grasp her…

CLAUDE MONET

46. Spring View from Sky Top

47. Morning Meadow Panoramic

BEAUTY

48. Sun Through Birches PRECEDING PAGE, LEFT

49. Laurel Above the Clove

To the attentive eye, each moment of

the year has its own beauty, and in the

same field, it beholds, every hour, a

picture which was never seen before and

which shall never be seen again.

RALPH WALDO EMERSON

50. Sky Top and Sunflowers

51. Clove Barn and Wildflowers

52. Awosting Falls, Boulders

The naturalist Loren Eiseley observed "if there is magic on this planet, it is contained in water." The Shawangunk Ridge is graced with an abundance of magical streams and waterfalls, including Awosting Falls and Verkeerderkill Falls, and their attraction is irresistible. Though the camera's silky rendering of flowing water captured more than the human eye could see, the elegant result is a perfect visual metaphor for how the scene felt to me.

53. Verkeerderkill Falls

54. Boulder and Stream Still Life #1

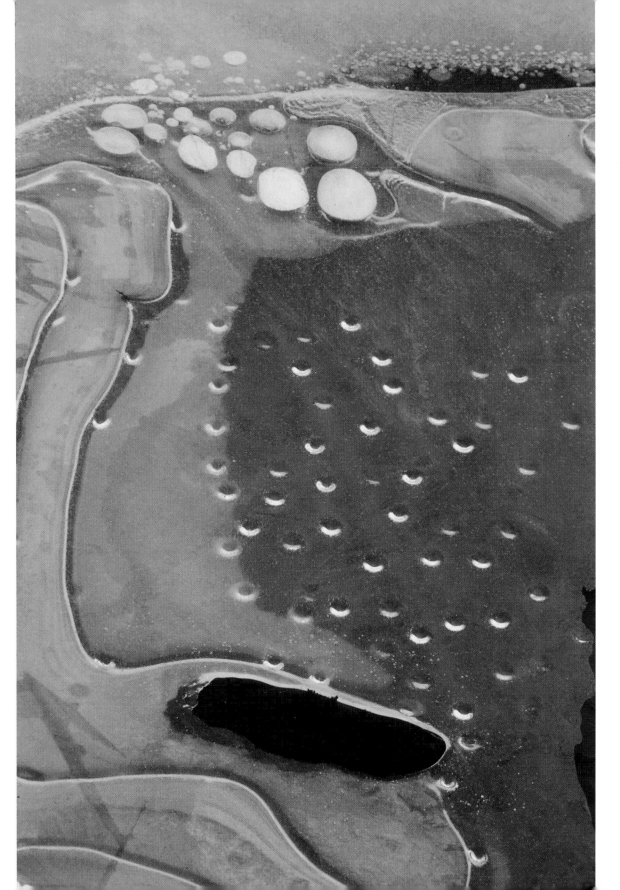

55. Ice Abstract

56. Oak Leaves, Summer

The poetry of earth is ceasing never.

JOHN KEATS

57. Red Maple Leaves, Detail

58. Detail, Autumn Blueberry Bush FOLLOWING PAGE, LEFT

59. Millbrook Autumn FOLLOWING PAGE, RIGHT

60. Clearing Morning Mist PRECEDING, PAGE 72

61. Peterskill Falls PRECEDING, PAGE 73

62. Spring Leaf Study PRECEDING, PAGE 76

63. Lone Tree, Clouds PRECEDING, PAGE 77

64. Late Autumn Sun, Lake Awosting

People viewing these photographs have remarked that they had been unaware until then of how beautiful the Shawangunk Ridge can be. This observation reminds me, in the words of composer John Cage, that "The artist's job is to pay attention."

On a visit to a friend's studio, I was struck by the beauty of a winterberry bush in his painting. Quite soon after that, I made this photograph. It was through his attentiveness that my eyes were opened to this scene.

65. Winterberry

66. Dickie Barre Spring. #2

67. Autumn Reflections, #2

68. Summer Sunset, Trapps

69. Sunset and Laurel, Above the Clove

70. Sunrise Over the Coxing Kill

71. Fern Detail

Nothing can be taken for granted: nothing is stereotyped.

The sections of an orange, the leaves of a tree, the petals of a

flower are never identical. It would seem that beauty

derives its charm from this very diversity.

PIERRE-AUGUSTE RENOIR

72. Moth Mullein

73. Spring Blossoms

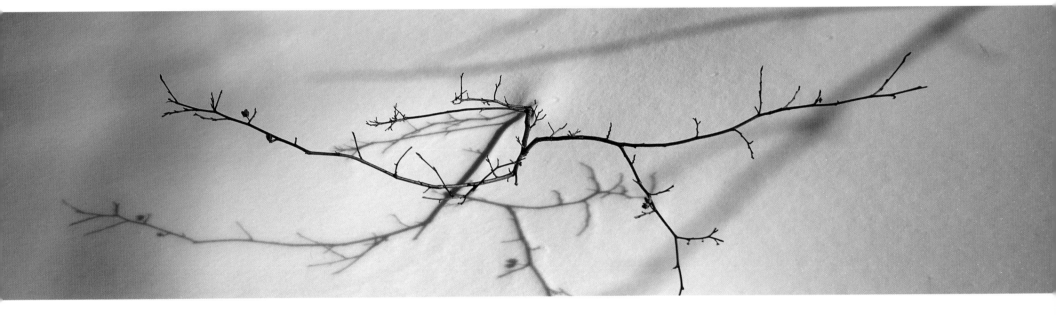

74. Winter Twig and Shadow Study

75. Autumn Stream Detail, Peterskill FOLLOWING PAGE, LEFT

76. Autumn View from Outback Slabs FOLLOWING PAGE, RIGHT

77. Winter Tree and Shadows

78. Winter Sun, Dickie Barre

79. Cliffs and Daisies

80. Spring Birch, Catskills

81. Winter Tree Shadow Abstract

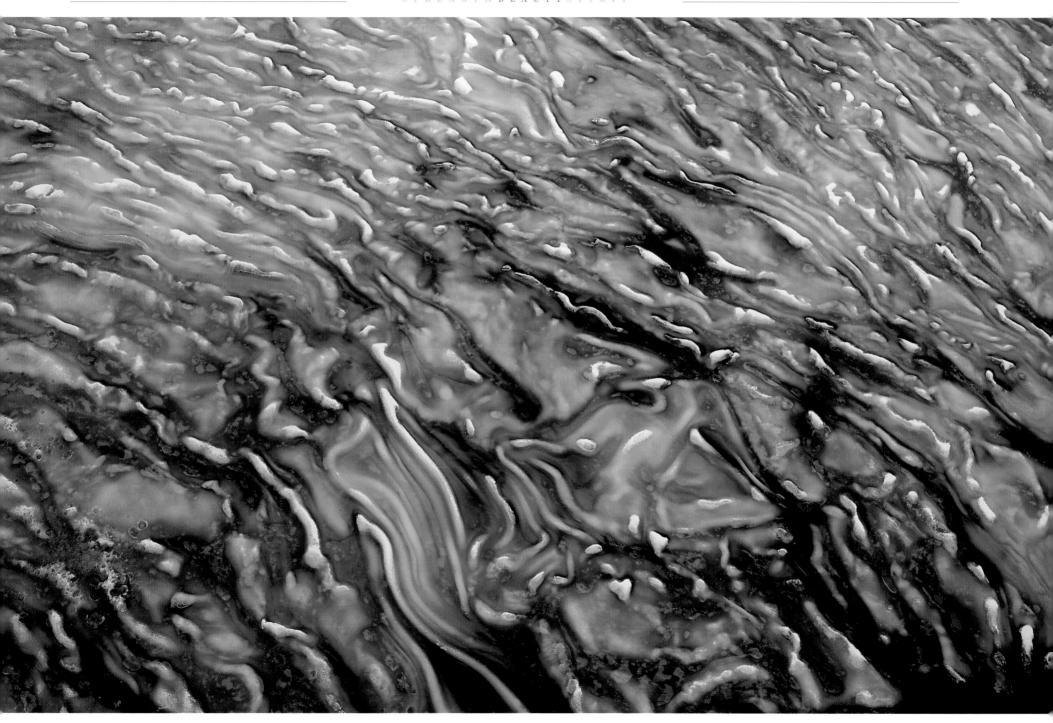

82. Ice Patterns, Rondout River

83. After the Storm, Humpo Marsh

We do not see nature with our eyes, but

with our understandings and our hearts.

WILLIAM HAZLITT

84. Winter Sun, White Pine, Mountain Laurel

85. Summer, Springtown Road

Spring along the Ridge is the most evanescent season of the year. Each day seems to yield a week's worth of changes in the appearance of the landscape. These fleeting scenes almost demand the power and veracity of the photograph to remind us of a delicate beauty that, in the heat and fullness of summer, we may question ever existed.

86. Near Spring Farm Trail

87. Dickie Barre Spring

SPIRIT

88. Orchard Pond Autumn PRECEDING PAGE, LEFT

89. Spring Trapps View

Over every peak

There is peace

In the treetops

You hear

Hardly a breath;

The birds in the forest are silent.

Just wait, soon

You will be peaceful too.

JOHANN WOLFGANG VON GOETHE

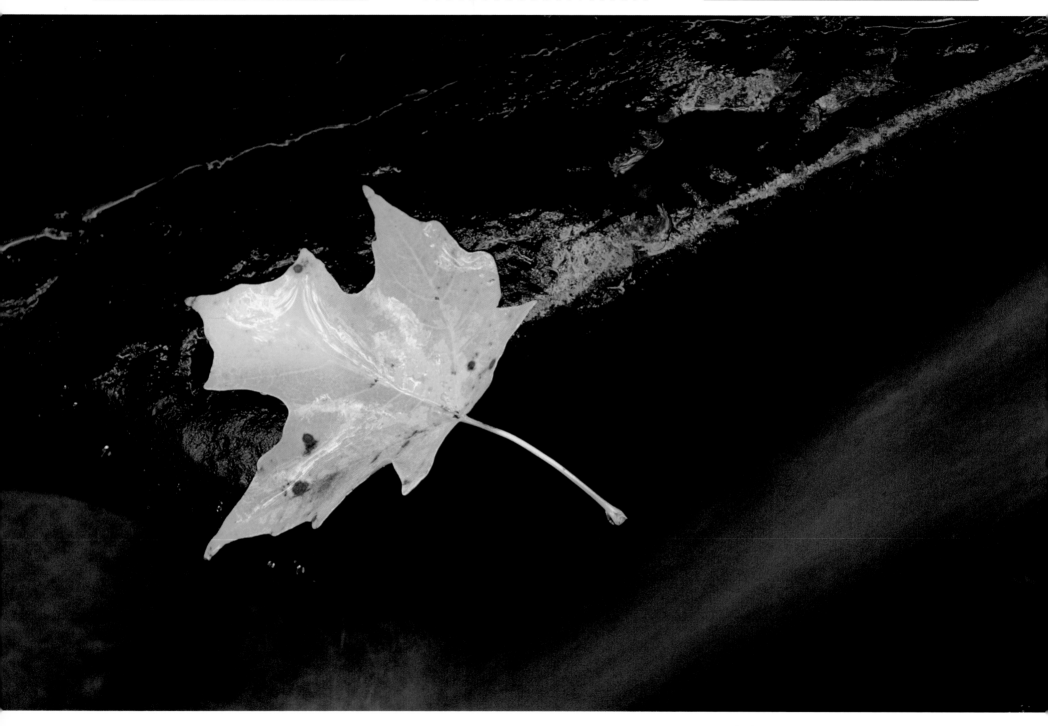

90. Leaf in Stream

91. Near Rhododendron Bridge

The art and craft of landscape photography is perplexing in its embrace of two competing principles: the desire to control what is framed and rendered on film and the equal but opposite need to recognize and graciously yield to the serendipitous, as I did when I encountered the faintly mysterious image of a split boulder in a bed of crimson blueberry bushes.

93. Split Boulder and Blueberry Bushes

94. Autumn Along the Upper Coxing Kill

95. Boulder in Stream

96. Winter Tree Study

97. Birch Copse Detail

98. Three Pines FOLLOWING PAGE

99. Glacial Erratic Above the Palmaghatt

100. Spring Trees Along the Wallkill

101. Split Rock Spring

102. Morning Above the Falls, Peterskill FOLLOWING PAGE, LEFT

103. Peterskill Summer Morning FOLLOWING PAGE, RIGHT

104. Flower and Tree

To me, these small images from the Mohonk Preserve and Shawangunk Ridge are bits of a jigsaw puzzle, randomly sought over the years and picked up wherever I've found them. And I'm surprised, when they're finally assembled, to see how many there are, how well they fit together, and how grand a picture they ultimately reveal.

105. Dry Streambed Study

106. Castle Point

107. Rock Abstract, Shingle Gully

108. Blue Hills, Evening View Toward Table Rock

Those things that nature denied to human sight, she revealed to the eyes of the soul.

OVID

109. Tree in Talus Slope

110. Autumn Panoramic, Awosting Falls

111. Morning Meadow

112. Clouds and Sun, Lake Awosting

No snowflake ever falls in the wrong place.

ZEN PROVERB

113. Winter Stream Study. #1

114. Trapps After Storm

115. Laurel Bog

116. Clove Spring

Many of the scenes captured here would be invisible to the casual observer of the Shawangunk landscape. In the case of "Catskill Spring View," the image represents a very small portion of the scene, condensed and brought closer by means of a telephoto lens. As a scientist explores otherwise unseen worlds by peering through a microscope, the photographer employs the tools of the medium to explore a landscape that the naked eye may not apprehend.

117. Catskill Spring View OPPOSITE

118. Along Lenape Lane

119. Winter Reflections, Lake Minnewaska

120. Spring Orchard, Sky Top

[We] esteem truth remote, in the outskirts of the system,

behind the farthest star…In eternity there is indeed

something true and sublime. But all these times and places

and occasions are now and here. God himself culminates

in the present moment, and will never be more divine in

the lapse of all the ages.

HENRY DAVID THOREAU

121. Summer Meadow

122. Summer Storm, Wild Mustard

I would like to express my deep appreciation to the people who helped make this book possible: Amy Hecht who not only designed the book and provided the title but was always a pleasure to work with despite having a fickle client; Bob Chase of RDChase Technology Group for his technical expertise and exceptional scans; Nina Smiley for her constant encouragement and wonderful insights; Glenn Hoagland, Debi Clifford and Vince Clephas of the Mohonk Preserve; Barbara Petruzzelli and Maurice van Swaaij for their superb editing skills; the landowners who graciously allowed me access to their property; and many others too numerous to mention whose contributions are also greatly appreciated. Finally, I would like to thank Ann Ryan for her support, encouragement and patience.